I'LL
TRADE
MY
SORROW

T0159384

I'LL TRADE MY SORROW

Trading The Pain Of Yesterday For A Journey That Frees Your Soul

Cynthia Primm

Orlando, Florida

I'll Trade My Sorrow
by Cynthia Primm

Published by HigherLife Development Services, Inc.
2342 Westminster Terrace
Oviedo, Florida 32765
407-563-4806
www.ahigherlife.com

This book or parts thereof may not be reproduced in any form, stored in a retrieval system, or transmitted in any form by any means—electronic, mechanical, photocopy, recording, or otherwise—without prior written permission of the author or publisher, except as provided by United States of America copyright law.

Copyright © 2009 by Cynthia Primm

All rights reserved
ISBN: 978-1-935245-09-4

Cover Design: Think Agency
First Edition
09 10 11 12 13 – 5 4 3 2 1
Printed in the United States of America

This book is dedicated to the memory of my mother, Muriel Parker Cole, and my sister, Courtney Candace Cole. Peace and self-love eluded them in this life, but I know that in Heaven they are complete in the love of our Heavenly Father.

Special thanks to Gloria "Lori" Radway, Jamie Nero, Susan Thornton, Dr. Alicia Pellegrin, EvaLynn Faucette, Barbara Jordon, and Dr. Dano Leli whose gifts of listening, counseling, and guidance have provided me hope for my future and the path to self-love.

Table of Contents

Introduction

THIS POETRY DETAILS MY journey through a life of turmoil, of reaching out and searching for love and acceptance, and never feeling like I would find happiness anywhere. You will read of my despair in these verses and also of my undying stubborn spirit of hope.

I was born to an alcoholic mother and an emotionally distant and violent father; I discovered early in my life that writing poetry helped quell the pain that always seemed to be overwhelming me. In those early years, and throughout the next two decades, I often thought the clouds would never clear.

Before each section of this collection, I offer a brief narrative of what was occurring in my life at the time of my writings. I want to bring hope to you if you face similar trials and to witness through my poetry the evolution of a person filled with despair to one filled with hope and a desire for inner peace and self acceptance.

In 1991, I wrote the following poem. Little did I know that this poem would foreshadow the changed life I have today.

> *New life*
>
> *can emerge*
>
> *from shadows.*
>
> *Voices*
>
> *can*
>
> *become song*
>
> *if*
>
> *in fleeting moments*
>
> *we believe.*

Learning, growing, and loving are continuous processes. Invest in yourself, listen to your heart, and hear the call to new life for you.

THE EARLY YEARS
Late 1970s—The Beginning

It Won't Last
Confusion
Music
No Place to Call Home
Let Me Fly
Me for Me
A Token of Your Love
Was It You?

My sister, Courtney Candace Cole, was born on November 21, 1970. *I remember* it was Thanksgiving Day. I was five years old at the time and was already confused by my mother's drinking and my father's volatility.

When Courtney was still a baby, *I remember* my mother and father's fighting as my sisters and I all piled into the car, my mother slipping on the ice and my father kicking her over and over.

I remember hiding under a bed with my sister Cheryl during another violent episode when the police came.

I remember my mother, in a drunken rage, driving erratically through four states, our St. Bernard dog and me held captive in the car. My mother was chasing my

3

father, who was in his tractor trailer, to return what she claimed was "his" dog to him. In the end, the police had to come and stop my parents' physical attack on each other at a gas station. The policeman who arrived on the scene told me to listen to my mommy and daddy.

I remember my father's being on the road most of the time; my mother out, or at home drinking; and my older sister Terry doing the best she could to take care of us all. My father had my mother committed. When she was released from the hospital he wouldn't let her come back home to us.

I turned 11 in 1976, and *I remember* that year my parents' divorce was final. Often I didn't even know where my mother was. During this period, there was a time when I didn't know where Terry was, either...

I remember when my sister Terry ran away and disappeared. Responsibilities for taking care of my sister Courtney and me fell to my sister Cheryl, who moved out in 1979. Then it became my responsibility to take care of my little sister. And just as helpless as I was before, I watched my father turn his anger towards Courtney. I still can hear the sounds of his brutality today.

I've included only eight poems from this time period. They are my first attempts at writing to ease the pain.

It Won't Last

I look into your eyes
And I see the hurt
You hide inside
And I realize how you feel,
How your world begins
To die.

The hurt is hard to bear
Rejection is no prize
Your mind begins to spin
No feeling in your eyes

Well, I have been there too,
My friend.
And I guess we've cried together
But eventually your heart will mend—
The pain can't last forever.

Confusion

Time is going by so fast
And yet so slow
In many ways
I have trouble distinguishing tomorrow
From today and yesterdays.

Memories mixed with thoughts
Of the future
Making me confused
My mind racing in many directions,
Tired and over-used.

This mass confusion continues
The end is not in sight.
I try fighting off the visions
That disturb my sleepless nights.

When will all this stop?
I feel as if I'm insane.
I try not to feel lonely,
My mind lost in the pain.

Music

The music dances in my head,
The rain comes tumbling down.
I need someone to come to me
And turn my world around.

The music rambles on
Reminding me of the past
But soon the melody will end—
Nothing ever lasts.

The music dances in my head,
The rain comes tumbling down.
I need someone to come to me
And turn my world around.

No Place to Call Home

The girl wearily crosses the street
Trying to fight the urge
To run and hug the next stranger
Until all her fears submerge.

She was left here just the other day
Alone and on the streets
With nowhere to go
And rejected by everyone she meets.

She was a little girl yesterday
Now suddenly she has grown.
A bitter woman now
With no place to call home.

She remembers people from the past
Memories that always last
Images are in her mind
Happiness is hard to find—

So she takes a bottle from the shelf
Trying to hide from her "real" self.
And soon she drinks her life away
Trying to forget the pain of yesterdays.

Let Me Fly

A little child runs and jumps
And thinks that he can fly,
And after falling and skinning his knee
He starts to cry.
The other children comfort him
And say "nice try."

He's just like one of us.

Our lives are filled with "nice tries"
And also big let downs.
You can tell by people's faces—
Smiles trapped with frowns.

We must all at times
Attempt to fly.
And if we fall,
At least we tried.
If our lives are too sheltered
Our wings will rust.
So let me fly...
I think you must.

A little child runs and jumps
And thinks that he can fly,
And after falling and skinning his knee
He starts to cry.
The other children comfort him
And say "nice try."

He's just like one of us.

Me for Me

When will I learn I am trapped on this earth?
I'm told what to do like a child at birth.
Big decisions aren't mine to make
And if I fail it will be because of your mistakes.

You won't let me run,
Say I must walk.
I can't speak my mind—
You won't let me talk.

You're wrapped up in what you want me to be.
I want the best, too.
Face reality.
I can't be a carbon copy of you,
I can't be your baby—
That time is through.
My Life is mine, not yours to keep
Realize that,
For this dungeon's too deep.

I love you, oh yes.
Please love me for me.
I can't always be what you
Want me to be.

A Token of Your Love

Don't let my wings be broken
When all my words have not
Been spoken.
I'm searching for a token
Of your love.

Notice me crying
While I am trying
To find you—
I don't know if I can take
What you are putting me through.
You must agree with me,
And let us be
Happy together.

Don't let my wings be broken
When all my words have not
Been spoken.
I'm searching for a token
Of your love.

Was It You?

Life is confusing me,
Messing with my mind.
Was it you I did see,
Or an image I'll never find?

I'm trying to understand
What's confusing me.
Did I enter a fantasy land,
Or was it you I did see?

Was it you? Answer me.
I'm so confused inside.
Was it you I did see,
Or was it just a lie?

The Teen Years
The Early '80s

I Am the Lonely One
If Only for Today
Optional Is Misery
Untitled
Game of Yesterday
No Sail or Rudder
D.S.
Nobody's Child
My 2nd Poem for DKW
My 5th Poem for DKW
Finds Me

In the early '80s, shortly after my fifteenth birthday, I came home one day from school to my father's telling me that I needed to find another place to live—immediately. He wanted to go back to his newest wife and she and I didn't get along. With only a trash bag to pack my belongings in, I called my sister Cheryl and she came and got me. I ended up living with many folks—my high school principal, an ex-boyfriend's mother—and finally settling in with my aunt and my cousin. My sister Courtney left with me, but my father came and took her back, separating the two of us one morning as we were preparing for church.

At the young age of fifteen, I was too immature to understand that I was not responsible for keeping those I loved safe—whether my mother or sisters during the violent times, or my little sister (who because of her age did not have a choice but to return to a world that would keep her soul mired in misery for the rest of her life).

The day I became emancipated through the courts, I went to collect the remainder of my items from the farmhouse where we grew up. This was the first (and last) time my father ever beat me, leaving me to feel as if I was not even good enough to protect myself. The following poems reflect a time of loneliness for me and my well-worn pattern of looking for acceptance outside of myself.

I Am the Lonely One

I am the lonely one.
Under the sun
Is my home.
I'm searching for someone
To love—
Could it be you?

I ask, *Could it be you*?
I need to know how you feel.
Is all that is happening real,
Or just an illusion?
It seems the sun always sets
To make way for a deep blue sky.
That is like a mirror of myself—
Just blue,
Unhappy.

Because I am the lonely one.
Under the sun
Is my home.
I'm looking for someone
To love—
Could it be you?

If Only for Today

I'll trade my sorrow for a smile
I'll sit and laugh awhile,
I'll play the games you want to play
If only for today.

I'll fly with you to Neverland
I'll dance with you and hold your hand,
I'll even try and understand
If only for today.

I'll hold you close
Then let you go—
I mustn't cry, I know,
For everything must go
Its own way.

And, if only for today
I will love you.

Optional Is Misery

After the love is gone,
And I find myself alone
I just can't bring to mind
The happiness I've known.

But then it's all up to me
Because optional is misery—
It's just something I can't see
When I am down.

After the love is gone
And silence creeps over me,
I find myself drifting
From reality.
And all around me seems strange—
I wonder why things had to change
Between you and me?

But then it's all up to me
Because optional is misery—
It's just something I can't see
When I am down.

Untitled

As each wave, however far
Finally reaches the shore,
So does my love
Finally reach you.

And as the waves weld themselves
To the shore,
So do I weld my heart
To you.

As the sun gently touches the sea,
So do we touch
And become one.

And even as the tides change,
And the sun sets,
Our togetherness will hold—
Because in the early hours
Of the morning
The sun will greet the sea.
And the kiss of life,
And the kiss of love,
Will find us
Once again.

Game of Yesterday

Trapped in a game of yesterday—
Hey, I don't want to play!
Too many broken dreams and fears,
Used-to-be's and tender tears
That never got wiped away
In our game of yesterday.

Old looks and special glances
Wrapped up in *just one more chances*
Love letters, rainy nights—
Oh, how it felt so right!
The nights never seemed to end
When you were my love and my friend…

Now it's just a game of yesterday
And I don't want to play
For now the game is through
And I've given up on you…

Game of yesterday
Here I begin to play.
I thought I could turn away
From you…

I can't.

No Sail or Rudder

The bitter current of life's swift sea
Seems to follow me
Turbulent waves slap me in the face—
A small craft drifting from place to place.

No sail or rudder to guide me,
Lonely, out on an open sea.
I ask, *What lies ahead*?
But not a word was to be said.

For a promise is not too sacred
To be broken
A guarantee is not a solid token
The bitter current of life's swift sea
Will carry me
To my destination—
Who knows where?
But I don't care, anyway.

For many a day I have drifted
And many a place I have seen—
But my lifelong aspirations
All seem to be hopeless dreams.

D.S.

Hatred in my head
Emptiness in my soul.
So much left to say—
Silence.

Beautiful stained glass,
Shattered.
My clenched fist,
Bleeding.
So much anger inside me
Over you.

Should I pick up the pieces
Of the glass?
Or let them stay fallen
And broken
Like me?
Can anything so shattered
Ever be put back together?

Hatred in my head
Emptiness in my soul.
So much left to say—
Silence.

Nobody's Child

She feels neglected.
She's nobody's child.
Everyone left her
In the world, cold and wild.

Once a little girl with parents
So happy and fine—
Corruption came
And many terrible times.

She was sent away,
She wasn't wanted anymore,
She wasn't needed,
They threw her out the door.

Like a piece of trash
They discarded her.
She wasn't good—
Caused too much of a stir.

She ruined their marriage.
That's what they say.
They treated her badly,
Then sent her away.

She's nobody's child.
She feels so alone.
Now she is settled,
Could this place become home?

It doesn't seem possible
Though she tries anyway—
But she lives with the fear
That again she'll be sent away.

When will security come for her?
She wants to stay here and live.
She's nobody's child
Searching for love.
That's all that she wants them to give.

My 2nd Poem for DKW

What I was going to give you
Lies packed away.
The wrapping paper has faded,
The items dusted with gray.

What I was going to say
Is locked up in my heart,
Never to be said—
Our love is torn apart.

What commitment I'd make,
What I was going to feel,
My love for you
Was something real.

I miss you so!
I cry through the nights.
I once had you here.
Once, things were right.

You left so abruptly—
I had no reason to know.
You thought I was smothering you—
You were planning to go.

I've never been able to love much in my life—
It was all so new to me.
I tried to give you all I could give.
And now we're something
That used to be.
And no words can reflect
The misery
Inside of me.

My 5th Poem for DKW

Darkness
Everything dark
Monotones in grays and black
Death's wind
Chills the spine.

Waiting for its prey
Lurking in the crevices
Of the night
The evil one is hungry.
And a broken heart
Will satisfy his empty mind.

Tears will cheer him,
And screaming cries of pain
And loneliness
Will excite him.

He is alive again
And dwells in the heart
Of man,
Who needs to escape.
The evil one helps him
And they become one—
Cold and desolate,
Dark.

Monotones in grays and black
Leaving the bright-eyed girl
With fear
And emptiness.

The evil one and his new conquest
Thrive on this—

And they roam and search for yet another man
Who needs to escape
From a bright-eyed girl.
Shattering her world
To quench their hunger—
Leaving darkness
And nothing more.

Finds Me

Sometimes I look back
And I'm not pleased
I see my past—
Not much at ease.

I try to look through untouched eyes
But my soul just won't respond,
For these eyes remember when they cried
And the pain still lingers on.

All the dreams could not protect me—
They will be gone in the end.
I often misplace the misery,
But it finds me once again.

It finds me when I run and hide—
It finds me when I'm deep inside
Myself,
Never letting me be.
Sometimes I look back
And I'm not pleased
I see my past—
Not much at ease.
When will I be free?

The College Years
The Late '80s

Pink and Gray
Jumbled Thoughts of Pain
But Not Your Heart
The Moon Without You
Winter

I LIVED WITH MY AUNT and my cousin until I grad-
uated from high school in 1983. During that time, I
had limited contact with my mother, my father, or my
sisters. The separation from the daily chaos of my family
afforded me glimpses of a "normal" life, but I remained
lost within myself and marred by my memories and
early messages of who I was, how to be loved, and how
to stay safe or not—by just not feeling anything.

I put myself through college, often holding down as
many as three jobs at one time. These jobs, coupled with
the help of scholarships and student loans, enabled me
to graduate and support myself, at least financially.

During those college years as I was wading through
the chasm of pent-up loss and grief, I first began counseling as well as dabbling in all things considered to be

"New Age." I was searching everywhere to try and stop the indescribable, lingering pain.

The college degree and the stint of living with my aunt in a normal environment had not cured what was wrong in my life—I still could not love myself. I was still seeking for love outside of me.

Pink and Gray

I'm just a form
Of pink and gray,
Like a grave
With flowers planted
And the petals pulled away.
To be blown
Into the wind
Unwillingly.

Jumbled Thoughts of Pain

Roll in,
Thunderous clouds.
Intrude on the
Silence
That has so
Devastated me.

The breeze
Clasps me in
Its hands—
And pushes me
Towards the edge,
Knowing that
I want to fall.

Take me in your arms,
Weeping willow.
Make me bend
In the breeze,
For I feel like
Breaking.

Found a body
By the water;
Thought it was me.
But I was mistaken
I was just wishing it
Was me.

The sky pours
Its sorrow
On my shoulders,
Adding to the weight
I already feel
Crushing me.

Rain on me, Rain.
Cleanse my soul
And make me
Good enough
For someone
To love.

People take out
Umbrellas
To shield themselves
From the rain.
But I want to feel
The rain.
For the pain
Is so devastating
That nothing matters—
Not even that I am
Getting wet…

Because who really cares?

But Not Your Heart

I could feel your eyes
Scanning me,
Touching me,
Candidly
Searching for clues—
As if you knew
Something inside me
Had snapped.

Perhaps it was my pride,
Knowing that you
Could love my body
But not my mind.
And hold my hand
But not my heart,
Treating me kind
Yet so aloof.
How cold your hands
Can feel
Sometimes.
And how I miss the warmth
They used to bring to me!

And now your eyes
Are scanning me,
Touching me,
Candidly
Waiting for a clue—
As to how I'm feeling.

Never really interested,
But somehow
Caring
With your eyes
And your hands...
But not your heart.

The Moon Without You

How big the moon is tonight!
Brightening the sky
With its bliss
Making my mind
Drift back to before,
To yesterday.

Star-filled sky,
Last warm breeze of fall
Ushering in the memories
Of the love
And the laughter we've shared.
Wishing to share the evening with you,
Feeling empty
As if the vastness
Of the sky
Fills my soul.

Yearning for the touch
Of your hand,
But feeling only
The breeze
Playfully brushing
Against me.

Lonely—
Lingering into the past—
Places we've shared,
Stopping for a moment
By the water.
Waiting—
As if I feel the memories
Will come alive again.

But knowing deep inside
You're gone.

Sharing the moonlight
With myself.
Making ripples
In the water
That reflect my thoughts.
Reaching continuously out
For the past.
Embracing it
On nights like these—
When I remember you.

Winter

Winter—
Cold
And threatening,
Lacing life
With ice
And forbidding
Warmth.

Snow,
Go away.
Winter,
Go away.
Let light
Intrude
Where ice
Has made
Such ideas
Impossible.

Let man's feelings flow,
And the heart so frozen
Thaw.
Let what was lost
Be found again,
Before ice
Made such ideas
Impossible.

The Next (Last) 20 Years

Lingering
Breathless
One View to a Kiss
A Pawn to Your Knight
Across the Wire
Thud
Your Field
Slowly Her Heart
Rising
Feel Me Fade
Footsteps
The Man I Love
Autumn
The Betrayal
In the Dawn the Darkness Comes
Little Bird that Sings
Let Me Rest
Against the Tide
The Edge
Rain Relentless
The Little Girl
Alone
Have a Nice Day
Where I Know You Well
The Path
Woman, Know It's True
New Life

It seems to me now, as I look back at my writing over the past thirty years, the emotions welling up in me have had more to do with sadness over how little I loved myself during those years than whether or not someone else loved me. I had disproportionately reached outside of myself for acceptance and love, but at some point I grew tired and finally began to understand that looking outside was not working to quell the deep chasm of loss inside.

During the twenty years when the following poems emerged, I devoted most of my energy to outward living: marrying, having three children, and developing a successful career. I went to counseling throughout this time, but still I hid most of my true feelings deeply within myself so as not to tap into pain that had built up inside.

I began writing less and less poetry, allowing myself no outlet for my real truths. Then in the first three years of the new millennium, I lost my sister Courtney when she was only thirty to her alcoholism, and my mother to cancer as a result of her destructive lifestyle. Life was pulling me down, the pain of my past stubbornly persisting, until *finally* I reached a point where I knew I had to focus on myself, my own needs, and work through the long-held pain that I had buried deep within just to keep breathing. It was time to try and start to live and to write again.

Lingering

Lingering in
goodbye—
leaves a longing
that marks the heart
with
hopes
unheard
of a life
together.

Lingering
in a kiss—
an embrace
meant for two,
only when she
closes her
eyes
to dream.

Throw away
the ties that
bind,
the walls
that close
your heart.
Let love in,
Let love go
its course.

For
lingering in
goodbye
leaves a
longing
that marks the
heart,
a sadness
that will
start
to unravel
what you dare
to dream
if you'd
close your
eyes.

Breathless

I want to
    breathe in
        the scent of
        your skin
wallow in the
    wild-eyed wonder
        that lies in wait
for guards
    dropped down
        unrestrained
for seconds.
    We could embrace,
        release a passion
            that would linger
                for a moment
                    in the winds that
                        mark the time
and space
    between us.
Rules meant to be broken
    for restless souls
        like ours.
The fire smoldering
    red-hot to touch.
        But oh the words
            run down the page
            trying to calm my
            wayward wonder
                at what your caress
                    would invite me to—
                a dance that could
                begin so slow,
                grasping at time,
                    trying not to lose
                        what used to be inside.

One View to a Kiss

So passionate—
your view to a kiss
such warmth to permeate
this quiet heart,
beating to be
heard.
Your view to a kiss
awakens the soul
left living a lost
memory
of
love.

A Pawn to Your Knight

You push me
to corners
where
blindly I turn,
forced to
abandon
what friendship
we'd had.
You
pull at my
necessity,
not letting
my view
or thoughts
or feelings
shine through.
Suddenly certain,
the ally in you
is temporal
at best—
for your own
purpose.
A pawn I am
to your knight—
cornered
and
running
for cover.

Across the Wire

When you called
my name
across the
wire,
my heart
stopped,
fluttered.
I felt
your breath
against my skin.

I shuttered,
shivered,
in the
cold
empty space
of phone lines—
entangled,
but living
apart.
Close to
my heart,
but still
your voice
echoes in my ears.

My heart stops,
beat-to-be-beat—
dial tones
erase what
was
until
we
meet
again.

Thud

You didn't
call me
back.
My pages
were left
empty,
unfulfilled—
wondering
if perhaps
you laughed
as each beep
came across.

Why
would I
imagine
something so
cruel,
yet possible?

Do I stop giving now?
Do I close the blinds and
draw the shades,
darkening my
heart?
It could have
been easy
for you
to take it all
from me.

Free falling
from that
cliff
seemed so
easy.
The wind
rushing through
my hair,
my heart
beating-to-be-beat...

And now
a resounding
thud echoes
from the hill.

It's over.

Why

I turn to you—
I want to know
why all of this is so?

Why does the
world spin
wearily
away
from all
that is good?

Tumultuous
tendencies
towards
emptiness
engulf
the chasm
of life's last breath.

Silence can
masquerade
the cries
of lonely
lives—
all reaching out
for reasons
to resolve
the depths
of hopelessness.

I turn to you—
I want to know
why all of this is so?

Why can't you
come and hold me
and turn the world
with love's warm glow
into something
we all know
can be so real
and full of light?

Oh, Lord!
The world cries out for you
to come and make all things new.
So much,
so lost
in signs of gray—
shattered lives have gone astray.
Wanting, waiting
for a time
when love will come
and heal all things undone.

I turn to you—
I want to know
why all of this is so?

Your Field

Dear God:
This is your field,
your land
I have been toiling through—
only now to realize
my harvest
is knowing you
and sharing your love
with others.

Forgive me
for the times
I have complained,
for I know your peace
and have shared
your peace
with others—
and know that
truly this
has brought me
closer to you.

I don't ever want to be
in a place
that's comfortable
but cold,
but rather
I'll stay in this field,
your land
and bring
comfort to those
in need.

Sustain me, Lord.
Help me not to complain,
to look for self-gain
when all that you
give
is more
than I could ever dream.

Amen.

Slowly Her Heart

Slowly her heart
closes in two.
It breaks
from the strain of the loss.
Head back, knees bent
she cries out to the sky—
why such loneliness,
why?

Tears that won't fall—
the waters icy edge
would cut her
soul.

She knows she must go on,
but in silence
she succumbs
to the numbing
cold
encircling all of the
memories.

His hands won't touch her
today.
No morning kisses
to find their way
into her dreams.

She sees him
silhouetted in
a window's pane,
walking further
away.

Unable to follow,
her heart
closes in two.
It breaks
from the strain of the loss.
Head back, knees bent
she cries out to the sky—
why such loneliness,
why?

Rising

I watched the sun
rise crimson red,
and at its solstice
felt your fire—
closed my eyes and spun around
and danced until my breath caught
inside my beating heart.
I know
you felt the sunrise too
in your bed
as if I lay beside you.

Winter breezes come to pass,
chilling windows frosted in
upon my hearth and heart—
your fire waits for me.
Even when 1932 Rowena
is just a memory,
I will lie in wait
and want
to feel your touch.

The moon rises now
so full,
gleaming,
bold,
so sure and true.
It leads me to
my dreams of you
and me.

Oh!
Set me free
from this waiting,
from dark to light,
this endless night
without you near.
And yet still
this distance does impart
a longing in my heart,
that although I know
you felt it too—
the sun, my sun
still rises
without you.

Feel Me Fade

Feel me fade.
Watch the breeze
swiftly push me
forward.
The edge,
obscurity
in all its glory
will clothe me
in its rapture,
glad to capture
the light inside.

Me,
fading,
waning,
waiting to catch
a glimpse
of night,
of comfort.
Obscurity
in all its glory
will clothe me
in its rapture.

Glad to capture
and keep
all that is left
of what I hoped to be—
locked safely,
tight
inside an orb
held far away
no longer in my grasp
to lose.
Feel me fade.

Footsteps

The wind whistled
as the rain swept
its brushing beat
against the ground,
cleansing the very path
from which we came.

Only footsteps out ahead—
the mooring of
familiar love.
Now dimly held,
its weight causing
a shift inside
us both.

Many suns and moons
did rise
while love so freshly
played
in tune with what we thought
we knew
together.

Now only footsteps out ahead
and no path to follow—
to regret—
yet a yearn to touch
the wind and rain-soaked path
is present still—
to know
that we once tread its street
together.

The Man I love

It is the man I love
with the rhythm there
echoing across the
rain-swept street.
I can hear it
as clear
as the day filled with sunshine,
when he loved me.

Hear the beat sway me
over the line
towards the edge
of such sweet
endurance
that I could not stop.
For wanting to love him
was as natural
as breathing.

It is the music
that haunts me still—
of his heart against mine
as we lay, swept into a dream
just on the edge of sleep.
I would hold his
hand in mine
and feel
complete.

Now alone,
I journey on
and let the rain
drop through my soul—
an emptiness that
he has given me
laced with grace
for my tender heart.

Still
a goodbye
nonetheless,
with music that follows me—
never to fade.
For our love was a melody as
natural
as breathing.

Autumn

Will the stain of you
fade from these autumn leaves
that surround me in the
late September sun?
Falling to kiss the ground
for October's festival
of art.

Tart taste of apple
lingers still,
memories of laughter
and the warmth of your smile—
of Providence Hill
Italian-full,
keeping me satisfied
into the night.

The breezes blow
and tussle my hair.
The leaves fall around me,
winter soon to chill—
covering in ice
that won't thaw.
The stain of you still
glistens through.

A memory that taunts,
a memory that warms—
a smile, a tear...
all the same.
Seasons come
and seasons go.
And, so like you—

a change so evident
that leaves so green
would burst to flame
falling to the ground...
then gone.

The Betrayal

It's the wind
in the trees
rattling my soul,
finding me
less than whole.

Breezing through,
lashing at thoughts
of you—
surrounding me
ever-hard.

To cleanse me
from the dust
of such mistrust
and haunting,
remembering that
you lied
and watched as
the hole inside
me opened
so that breezes
ever-cold
would chill my soul.

For so long
I had wanted,
and waited,
and had
a song to fill me
full—
and now feeling the
breezes pull
at me,
push me still.
I want to
run until
I can no longer
feel your betrayal.

In the Dawn the Darkness Comes

In the dawn the darkness comes
as she opens her eyes to the morn,
struggling to feel the sun
dance against the storm.

Was rain that sent her to her slumber?
Weariness, like a cloak
that held in all the light she had,
and left her without hope.

Waking to another day,
she wears a mask to hide
all she has lost—
and the fading of light
no one can see inside.

Little Bird that Sings

Such a sadness
in your song—
fair bird who sings
without
the sunlight
beating at your
breast.

Warm days of
spring will
come
to dry
your drowning
coat of dreams.

Look to the
light, my friend.
Feel the
warmth of
tomorrow...

for little bird
of sorrow,
the warmth will
come.

Let Me Rest

Let me rest
in the corner
of my sleep,
pressed
tightly
in the shadows
of my mind.

Relentless morning
filled with need
paws at me,
unrestrained.
The shadows hide me,
if only for a time.

Let me rest in the corner
of my sleep,
wake me not
to start another day.

Too much pain,
too much sorrow
circles me
and the only comfort
is this corner of mine.

Against the Tide

I am worn down
by the world
and its ways.
Winds that blow
such uncertainty
when I long for
knowing.

All that I am,
all I've meant to be—
to have,
to give—
constrained,
contained.
A hidden light
inside of me,
wanting to shine
to awake to a world
that is not against me.

Tiring easily,
as I have traveled so long
against the tides
and waves that chafe
my soul and leave me
out of breath,
standing.
In spite of
the storm,
I struggle
to see

all that I am,
all I've meant to be—
to have,
to give—
constrained,
contained.
A hidden light
inside of me,
wanting to shine
to awake to a world
that is not against me.

The Edge

Falling
ever so slowly,
gradually to the edge.
Looking down
becomes easier
than looking up.

Hope does not abound
in darkness.
Light cannot enter
when on the edge
and time runs out.
It's over.

Why must the sun set,
the rain fall,
the moon rise,
the thunder roll?
Why must the waves
continue to beat
on this shore
of my heart?

I do not see your face,
I do not hear your call—
I am alone on this edge.
You will not come.
Separated and so different,
we are.
When looking down becomes
easier
than looking up,
hope does not abound.

We circle round the truth
and now only darkness
silences and stills
my heart.
From the start,
from the very beginning
I have been alone....
and alone
I will remain.

Falling
ever so slowly,
gradually to
the edge.

Rain Relentless

Walking in the gray,
no blue skies—
the sun is for another day.
Rain relentlessly
beats at my heart,
suppressing joy
and hope
for tomorrow.

Such a narrow hall!
Confined am I—
I cannot see
around the stairs,
climbing for what seems
an eternity
to who knows where...
to who I am.

Wanting to cry,
to run,
to escape this gray
where the sun is hidden
for another day.
And the rain
relentlessly
beats
at my heart,
turning it to
stone.

The Little Girl

Talking to myself,
talking in my sleep
unable to stop the flow
of words,
of thoughts,
of dreams suppressed.
Who is she,
that girl I left
to die?

I think I liked
her laughter,
her passion,
the power of her
smile.
Lighthearted
unencumbered
playful
willing
wishful
without discordance—
alive.

Dancing
writing
singing
loving
sharing...
daring
to dream.

Talking to myself,
talking in my sleep
unable to stop the flow
of words,
of thoughts,
of dreams suppressed.
Now vividly prodding me
not to let go
of her hand,
my hand—
my heart,
my life.

Alone

I am saddened by the wind
rustling through my soul
finding all the holes
left unfulfilled.

Of places changing,
and faces fading,
and hope remaining
elusive still.

A melancholic heart have I—
a cold night's call,
a moonlit cry,
waiting for the
dream to die...
so I can fade.

Quiet as a rising dawn
dew that kisses my eyes to close,
holding on to all I know
of sorrow
in a life unbowed.

Of places changing,
and faces fading,
and hope remaining
elusive still.

I stand against the raging storm—
letting go,
keeping warm
tightly wrapping around myself—
alone.

Have a Nice Day

Have a nice day.
No invitation—
you pushed me away.
Made your choice
aloof and cold
chilled my soul
and offered
less and less...
oh, but with
a smile
Have a nice day.
As if I were
a stranger
in danger—
with you
always
a wolf
in sheep's garb
with a smile.
Hidden barbs
that pierce me
through—
looking at you,
hearing you,
seeing you.

Screaming
inside my head
just wanting
to be felt, seen, kept—
not pushed away
Have a nice day
he said.
Still fighting, I—
ridiculous to deny
that all along
you used me
and use me
still…
until I become
strong enough
to walk away,
unfulfilled.
But finally,
yes finally,
free.

Where I Know You Well

One more look
for you to see
what I hide inside of me
behind the smile
a well-hid tear—
you will not find
sunshine here.

A darker rain
it falls to fill
this chasm in
my heart so still.
The beating long ago
did slow.

One more look
and you will know
it's in this midst
I love to dwell.
It's there I find
I know you well.

A childish wonder,
a lover's dance—
a different twist
of circumstance
could change my sorrow
to a prayer.
Will I find you
standing there?

Or will this ode
find you afar?
Will thoughts and feelings
run ajar?
Will the chasm's
rain depart
a steady murmur
to my heart?
It's in this midst
I love to dwell.
It's there I find
I know you well.

The Path

In mid-air
not in my will.
Carried in your loving arms
scared, not knowing yet
But, still
your love will keep me
far from harm.

Blind to what is just ahead,
straining as I start to dread.
But I have faith to rest
assured
that any path my feet will take,
your grace
will help me
to endure.

Father, Abba, Savior, Friend—
you are so gracious
as my guide
let not my feet ever
leave this path
Where I can travel
by your side.

Woman, Know It's True

In the moments
of remembering,
a voice so still
did whisper
Seek the truth.
Find the answer
in your song,
singing up
from your soul.
Know the answer—
it is true
to your
heart,
and the wisdom
that follows
will fold you
in its arms
and hold you
still
as you seek
to see
the light coming forth
to warm you.

The poetry contained in this book was written over a thirty-year period. Putting these words on paper has freed my soul. I have learned to love myself, to celebrate what makes me uniquely me, and to pursue what makes my heart dance.

If you have found bits of yourself in these writings, I encourage you to continue on your own road to self-discovery and healing. Many mentors and counselors have provided guidance to me on my journey, just as there will be people around you who will assist you in your personal journey when you are ready.

Ultimately, you will not find the answers outside of yourself, but within, which means you are in complete control of the momentum. Are you ready? Are you brave enough to move through and away from the lingering pain to a new life?

New life
can emerge
from shadows—
voices
can
become song...
if,
in fleeting moments,
we believe.

Forever writing, feeling, breathing, searching, living
Compilation created 2008
A look back
Don't forget to DREAM

LaVergne, TN USA
28 December 2009
168238LV00001B/1/P